Secret of Success: Personality

I0490986

Secret of Success: Personality

Who am I? What do I want?

Translated from the original German

by Elizabeth Hormann

The way to a successful, autonomous future through
systematic character building

Dr. Norbert Hermann

Bibliographical Information from the German National Library:

The German National Library has recorded this publication in the German National Bibliography; detailed bibliographic data are retrievable on the Internet under http://d-nb.de

For questions and suggestions:

norbert.hermann@go4business.org

(German Version) 1st Edition 2019, March 2019

Design inspiration Rita Hermann

Character drawings and cover design Max Beindorf

FOR RITA

who is lovable unconditionally because
she is who she is

Disclaimer:

Even though the information presented in this book on developing potential, was researched to the best of my ability and in all conscience and suggestions for continuing education and further development were expressed, at this juncture, it is pointed out that all information is subject to correction. Neither the publisher nor the author assume responsibility for any damage occurring from the use of this book, in particular from the use of the exercises and the procedures described.

ACKNOWLEGEMENTS

I THANK all of those who have helped with the development of this book.

I also thank my mentors, who believed in and promoted my abilities, who, through their knowledge and the sharing of their experiences, spared me many detours and enabled me to have much success in my life, through which I am able today to support other people with my life experience, to achieve their goals

In particular, I also thank Prof. Dr. Detlef Beeker, who inspired me to write this book and was able to give me valuable tips for dealing with the publishing sector.

Thanks too to the designer, Max Beindorf, who created the character figures in this book and for my presentations in my seminars. He implemented my vision for this perfectly.

FORWORD

Congratulations! You have arrived; You are already a winner because you are investing in the development of your own personality, even if it is with this schematically structured and concise workbook.

Thereby, you have already declared the firm belief in progressing via practical knowledge and stand out from the masses, who often want to progress without doing the right things for it.

I believe that, through the contents of this book, you will be enabled to have clarity of thought in relation to your goals and, thus, a focus on utilizing the right opportunities is possible. By doing this, you can develop your personal prospects competency. Primarily, the following questions will be answered.

- *How do I get the right orientation to have lifelong success?*
- *What is the purpose of my life? Which path is the right one for me to achieve my vision for my life?*
- *How can I manage my life? Instead of "I must" towards "I want to"?*

How do I obtain a clear vision of my goals and how do I achieve this with peace and serenity?

- *How do I recognize my personal, useable opportunities and how do I differentiate them from opportunities that are not usable for me?*
- *How can I get to know my personal route to making decisions so as to be able in the future to detect opportunities accurately and quickly and, thereby, to be able to recognize and use opportunities more effectively?*

How do I create a purposeful, successful and happy life for myself?

For over a year, our team worked on this book, launching the series, which started with this book on **Go4BetterLifeConcept** *and on the seminar* **Go4BetterLife** *and incorporating both university and experiential knowledge about successful people from the practice into this book and the seminar.*

The results of this work are, firstly, this book and also a seminar on the topic of personality with groundbreaking development tools for developing your personal prospects competency or, more explicitly, a system for positive change! Ultimately, this serves to steer our habits in a positive direction since we perform a large percentage of our daily activities habitually.

If we build a workable system to target positive habits in our lives, it is more effective and efficient to change our behaviors through this in the direction of personal success in order to build a successful future.

Here too, with the useable knowledge from this book, you are laying the necessary mental foundation, since you now know a system for developing your personality structure!

Consequently, the contents of this book serve to develop a necessary personality structure for successful people, through which you will become more aware of your own abilities and skills and, thus, be able to make decisions more quickly and effectively. You will be supported in this with the useful exercises that follow and the experiential knowledge of many successful people in your search for groundbreaking possibilities for a successful life.

I wish you much energy and drive for the hours that follow so that you can discover a great deal for and about yourself and put it into practice. You have it in your power!

I hope you will enjoy learning this and succeed in applying this knowledge.

Dr. Norbert G. Hermann

Table of Contents

Introduction

Target Focus: Success

You would always have to be a bit "other than the others! (OTO) to want success, to be "rich". Also, you must constantly work more than others, read more books, go to more seminars than others, deal more with your own abilities and skills than others. Yes, all this while we possibly "wait" actively for our success.

It is vital that we orient our target goal towards success so that we enable *ourselves* to experience our vision of our future!

The current research indicates that the characteristics of successful personalities are similar.

These people are mostly open for new things, impartially acting flexibly, often extroverted, mostly ambitious and, furthermore, with strong psychological characters with (more or less) little self-doubt and, with increasing age and experience, have a special and mostly positive charism, especially from the perspective of the general populace.

Tool for success: Personality development

The structure of this book is primarily focused on the goal that you know yourself well, that you develop a clear self-image, that, by building on this, you acquire greater self-confidence – this through a clear, comprehensible structural knowledge of our personality and a precise vision of our own future.

How to use this workbook

At the start, we deal with initial reflections on your **mindset**, that is, with your mental attitude and various possible **ways of thinking**, which either block or are essential for our success. Building on this, you can draft an initial plan for your **life vision** with the four-leaf clover method.

Afterwards, it is crucially important for your future personality development that you learn about your **potential** in Chapter 3

Further then, in Chapter 4, also your individual **values**, because you orient your decisions towards them and these can unconsciously influence your actions strongly.

Subsequently, you have the possibility to determine through a **SWOT Potential Analysis,** your major strengths and weaknesses, as well as your opportunities and risks, in order to be able, in Chapter 5, to discover your **mission**, your usefulness for third parties.

Furthermore, in the following Chapter 6, this book deals with our **basic beliefs**, because they too have a *decisive* effect on our unconscious dealings and, thus, represent a significant factor for success.

Chapter 7 is important for you because you are now given an idea of how you can bring about the necessary **behavioral changes** for you can only achieve your desired success through a change in your personality.

Finally, in the last working chapter, you will be able to undertake a compressed fine tuning of your life's vision and to formulate yourself and your mission into a **success-pitch**.

Now you know precisely who you are, what you can do and what you want!

After the finale, useful tips related to the development and influencing of the topical area and **growth drivers** follow as success-accelerating measures.

Personality Development as a Success Factor

A good and indispensable prerequisite for personal success is to deal with your own personality development, primarily with your own personality growth! This offers the possibility of developing your potential and, thereby, your own personality.

Knowledge of oneself is the basis for focused personality development. Thus, I must first ask myself some questions so that I comprehend was influences me, the criteria[1] on which I make decisions, what I ultimately believe and what is important to me.

Thereby, with these and further questions, I get to the point that I can define my roots and my current standpoint in order to build upon them and to be able to begin, in a purposeful way, with my further personality development.

Out of the comfort zone and into the growth zone

Growth in your own personality development, in your personality unfolding, can only be generated if we leave our familiar comfort zone and change into the initially uncomfortable growth zone to enable to our personality to unfold.

---

[1] Values, opinions, convictions, basic tenets, etc:

This term (**comfort zone**) can be understood in this connection as an area of private or professional life, which is characterized by comfort, a large measure of freedom from risk, and security. Long-term, this zone also means stagnation or even reverting to an ever smaller personality structure. Growth in this area is fundamentally not possible.

Under growth zone, it is understood in this connection as a loss of security by stepping into an area where more risk and more energy are required, often with fear of change and the unknown. But it is also the area, which enables us to grow into our new, unknown challenges. Comfort is, thereby, out of place. Anxiety and pain must be overcome!

What's behind all this? If things are going to change for the better, we must first become better ourselves. For only then, when we constantly develop ourselves further, will we become the personality, that can actually live out our dreams in the future!

To this end, we must achieve another level of thinking and personality than those where we find ourselves at the moment.

A simple example: Imagine that you wanted to enjoy a better view and that there is a staircase available for that. If you really wanted this, you would have to climb the stairs, step by step, even if it is exhausting.

Whoever wants to grow, must therefore, leave your comfort zone! Overcome your laziness. Accept the effort involved.   Only then will you be able to enjoy a better prospects in the time required.   Only then will you have reached your goal!

Whoever want to grow, must, therefore get out of his (or her) comfort zone! And into the growth zone! You can only win outside of your comfort zone.   For only here lie the opportunities, your possibilities and wait for your proactive implementation.   Only here can you actually make use of your opportunities.

On the next page, there is the graphic "Leaving the comfort zone" so as to land in the growth zone.

Description of the picture: Everyone must leave the comfort zone as soon as he/she wants to evolve. This only happens through action. Hereby it should be noted that the pain factor must be overcome (i.e. comfort or anxiety, etc.) in order to land in the growth zone.

Thereby, everyone grows *with* or *through* his/her experiences. Through actions and the experiences that result from this, everyone can develop his/her potential. The individual personality can then be more consciously perceived and developed and individual personality growth occurs.

If one does not act and stays in the comfort zone, there is basically no growth possible.

Chapter 1 My Mindset

Thoughts are powers which either allow us to prevail over or also – depending on which level of thinking – we have – we go under. Success, wealth and personal profile occur first in our heads in the form of thoughts. You already know this: Thoughts are powers, which seek a way to fulfillment!

Basically, everyone can program the unconscious for success. Therefore, every person can and must set certain consistent individual, ideal, financial and professional goals, so that the subconscious can be a helpful power in achieving his/her personal goals.

Now, let's begin to work on your personality: First we begin to build the foundation, in which we start at the point of vision.

Using your own vision, focus on your future. The focus should, for example, comprise about 10 years: What should happen in ten years, how do we imagine our Big Picture?

Before we begin with the exercises in our workbook, we should first question our thoughts – on a meta-level however. This means on a high level to grasp how our thinking occurs currently and, generally speaking, on which level during the day, we find ourselves conceptually, so that we can better evaluate and steer ourselves.

During the day, every person will reside in each of the three following levels of thought being described.

However, you will only be successful in implementing your life vision and your personal goals, when you have managed to be in the uppermost thinking level (and, thereby, in the zone of creativity) as often as possible.

As soon as you have gotten acquainted with and internalized the content of the various thinking levels, you will easily be able to estimate, with the help of the various parameters, what your current contact persons, your personal influential people, are thinking now.

Thus, with those persons with whom you deal daily, you can now better identify and, thereby, assess their way of thinking in order, for instance, to consciously become independent from negative influences and distance yourself.

On the other hand, your can join company with people who bring you closer to your vision and support you on your way to your personal success through their creative ways of thinking.

Your personal mindset is, thus, an important factor for success. Your mental approach and the way you deal with your own thoughts is decisive for success or failure!

Bringing about clarity in thinking

It won't work without the three frequently cited "C"s of success: Clarity, competency and consistency!

First of all, in our development into a successful personality, it is not without reason that we must achieve clarity. Clarity about our WHY, clarity about our basic beliefs and values, as well as clarity about our intermediate goals on the way to our individual success!

Moreover, with respect to our path, we should also attain clarity about the necessary activities on our side and those of our future networks, as well as what price for what goal, in the form of doing without, we are prepared to accept and whether we are prepared to provide the required trade-off.

The clarity about this puts us in the position of being able to implement corrections to our path or even our goal if necessary. Consequently, we can deal with the HOW for our path, that is, with the necessary substance of the action!

As soon as you are clear about how the various ways of thinking can contribute to your personal success, you can begin to deal more and more with things which can bring you further personally.

Things that you don't have to do, but rather, want to do.

It is now more efficient if you do not fill your valuable time with things that you don't want to do, because that does not get you any further!

For the most part, occupy yourself predominantly during the day only with the things that you actually think are important and need for achieving your goals

For this purpose, there are many levels and areas on the creative thinking level to scrutinize, so that a sustainable success can be brought about. As already described, this should happen at the highest thinking level, at the creative, the imaginative thinking level!

At this point, let's first go into our options with respect to the various conceptual cultures.

Let's look now at a simple classification of our conceptual culture, thus (also looking at) various conceptual levels. Hereby, we can organize our thoughts in the future in various ways of thinking. Furthermore, we can begin to influence our thoughts and, thereby, our subconscious in such a way that we program a success-promoting way of thinking, through a correct conceptual world.

At the same time, we put ourselves in the position to recognize which of our blockades are in the form of false thinking and can take targeted countermeasures.

This happens through awareness and use of the knowledge about various levels of thought.

Let's look closely now at the thought level and its differences in order, in an initial step, to be better able in the future to steer our thoughts by scrutinizing our thoughts and asking in which thought level we find ourselves during our thinking process.

Furthermore, in the next step, we will also be able to better judge our reference persons.

On each of the next pages, one thought level is described. In general, it should be noted that:

"The law of resonance always confirms our own thought level"

Different Mindset, different behavior!

Your Decision!

Thought culture and thought resonance

Now let's keep in mind the various thought levels

Destructive level:

1. The lowest level of thought is the position of destruction, which we can take with our thoughts. This will be recognizable through the following characteristics and will be presented here as the lowest basis of thought:

(negative emotional environment)

a.) Internal attitude: "Everything is negative!"
b.) In practice vis-a-vis your environment:

On this thought level, you find problem thinkers with many doubts, which indicates a fundamentally negative attitude.

Here, there is negatively biased thinking. Furthermore, this expresses itself in complaints, criticism, recrimination, prejudice, the others are to blame etc. People who can be found primarily in this thought position, do not willingly leave their comfort zones, for leaving it means giving way to their comfort and their anxiety. Frequently not even an attempt is made but rather there is a search for an excuse for why something does not work.

The retaining level

2. The middle level of thinking is the position of **preserving the status quo** and of defense, which we can seize upon with our thinking. This is recognizable by the following characteristics and is presented as the middle thought basis:

(positive world of emotions)

a.) Inner attitude: "What we have, should be preserved!"

b.) In practice vis-a-vis your environment:

With this level of thought, it is about retaining and defending what is available and hanging onto the current state.

Hereby, this thinking level is characterized by anxiety about loss influencing the negotiations and therefore, that which has been achieved is held onto.

That which has been achieved should not be let go of because the past confirms the current state.

The new and that which is different from "normal everyday life" is accepted only with difficulty or not at all. This also makes itself noticeable in that, for example, that which is available, is maintained.

At this level of thought, hanging on to earlier success is predominant.

Sometimes, this thought level is not entirely understandable because people at this thought level believe that they can leave everything the way it was, thereby staying situated in their comfort zone but, at the same time, entertain the hope that something will change.

It should also be emphasized here that we can feel well in this zone, but will not, however, grow since we are not prepared to leave our comfort zone.

Creative Level

3. The highest level of thought is the position of **creation**, which we can occupy with our thinking. This will be recognized through the following characteristics and will be presented here as the highest basis for thought:

(positive emotional world)

a.) Internal attitude: „Positive Meta-Perspective!"

b.) In practice vis-a-vis their environment:

Thinking at this level is characterized by solution-oriented positive thinking.

People at this thought level have no or only few doubts. Also, they have no anxiety or qualms about starting new projects. Furthermore, people in this mindset see problems more as a chance.

Rather, they begin to develop something new creatively, characterize themselves through positive action for the benefit of a third party, have an innovative way of thinking and have an idea-rich mindset, through which they can approach new situations without biases.

Letting go of previous successes is possible and doable. Cooperative thinking replaces confrontational thinking.

Additional remarks on the thought levels outlined

Basically, at this point, it must be clearly expressed that none of these thought levels are fundamentally good or bad nor do they have positive or negative connotations.

On the contrary, every day we find ourselves in all thought levels because our feelings also influence our thinking. But your feelings should not be ruler of your thoughts and your activities. You must be ruler over your thought if you want to achieve your goals. Thus we become the ruler over our future experiences because, thanks to this knowledge, we are in a position to evaluate these experiences at an intentionally other thought level.

The goal of the focus of our thought level is, first of all, that we recognize this thought level, both in ourselves as well as in our environment. Furthermore, that through this knowledge and our intentions, we are in a position to voluntarily focus our thinking on the creative thought level.

The goal of the cognitive, i.e., of the conceptual understanding of the thought levels must also be worked out so we are in the position of being able to recognize the thought level in which we currently find ourselves. With this, you can recognize your subconscious running program and your subconscious approach. This is so that we can consciously select a thought level and can consciously choose another thought level in the upper levels of this model, in the creative thought level. Consequently, knowledge about this thought level is desirable because it is focused on your personality development and can have influence on your personal success.

Your thinking today is also a result of your previous experiences. Thus, people who primarily think in the lower thought level, in the destructive level, have often been through bad experiences and think that the world is the way that reflects their experiences. This is because they themselves have had bad experiences or these were passed on to them.

Often, the people at this thought level stand out through their destructive manner with respect to their environment vis-à-vis things as well as other people.

Similarly, people, who are mostly situated on the thought level of defense, often think about the possible risk that could accompany a decision to act and concentrate more on the risks than on the opportunities of the new possibilities. As a result, security thinking then also takes priority and that which is already present is protected by rejecting change and something new.

If people think in the upper, imaginative, creative level, they set their potentials free through this kind of thinking and how they perceive their environment,. This kind of reflection motivates people to rise above themselves.

With this way of thinking, trust as a value is uppermost in the ranking.

1st Milestone – Thought level

This is your first of twelve milestones
in this book In the future, you
will know how to consciously
dictate the direction towards
a creative thought level.

You also need creative, imaginative thinking for processing and developing your personality structure in this book so that you can achieve the maximum success for yourself.

You will always find further milestones in this book after each section. The important educational content is recorded for you there. Please work on the educational content systematically – one after the other – because all of the points build on each other exactly in the sequence you find in the text and end with the final exercise.

Chapter 2 My Vision

What is a life vision and why is this important?

> *"He who doesn't know where he wants to go, should not wonder later if he arrives somewhere else."*
>
> **Mark Twain**

A life vision gives us a clear view of how our life, with all its future living conditions and our living environment should look. The vision expresses our own concept of how we want to live in the future and what we want to achieve in our life.

"A vision is an intellectual anticipated success"

As with a puzzle, this shows the big picture. By contrast, goals are the appropriate puzzle pieces. And the strategy answers for us the question of HOW we can best put together our puzzle in order to complete the big picture.

If we have first set down our personal life vision in writing, it makes our life easier because, through the orientation provided, clarity of mind prevails, the necessary goals can be laid down and implementation can begin.

Furthermore, opportunities can be more easily identified, which can be beneficial to us on our way to our life goals.

Moreover, a vision also gives us orientation. With a life vision, we are in the fortunate position of being able to make decisions more easily because we now know our personal direction.

In addition, through this, we can recognize opportunities which enable us to act purposefully instead of having to react in an uncoordinated way.

On this, now the following example:

"Whoever aims at nothing, does not encounter anything."[2]

First imagine you were on a meadow and had a bow in one hand and in the other hand an arrow that you want to shoot. In the quiver on your back, there are more arrows. Thereby, you are in a position to shoot several arrows.

In one case, you fire your arrow off with full power, but without a goal.

In the next example, you fire again with full power, but have a goal that you are aiming for. This time, your shots go astray a couple of times, but also hit the target a couple of times.

---

[2] Lao Tse, general worldly wisdom.

Let's assume that the arrows symbolize your talents. Then, in the first example, you would have shot all of your talents indiscriminately without any effect. In the second example, however, you would have achieved the goal – precisely because you had a target focus.

> ➤ Impulse 1 "Thought-provoking focus on the target"

Compare the pictures and ask yourself which situation more likely applies to you!

Without a target focus, I squander my talents. I am unsuccessful

With a target focus, I use my talents expediently. I am successful!

Why develop a life vision?

After this example, it will also be clear why we must deal with our vision, with our big goal,

Now, how do I develop my own personal life vision?

First, a couple of important insights that we must consider ahead of time.

Haven't you also often observed this? With people who have already dealt once with the finite nature of their own lives, have often been confronted with life situations, such as, after a serious illness or death in their immediate surroundings, often live a changed, intensive and more fulfilled life! To express it in the words of Mario von Andrade:[3]

"We have two lives and the second begins when you

notices that you only have one!"

---

[3] Poet and author, essayist and musicologist, San Paolo, 1993-1945

As a result of this situation, these people have frequently given thought to what should be of significance in their lives, have, therefore, actually begun to *consciously* develop their own personal life vision.

Moreover, these people with their own life visions have achieved a clear picture of their goals.

A clear vision allows for clear results to occur because we then have an idea of what we will have in the future and who we want to be, how and with whom and in which environment we want to live.

Visions are a self-fulfilling prophecy, an anticipated view of the success in our possible future life. Therefore, we need a clear idea of how that future should look.

Only then, do we have a chance to be as successful and happy in our lives as we want to be, because we know that our activities are always a step in the right direction.

And only then are we in a position to optimally recognize our chances and to use them to attain our personal goals.

My personal design for my life vision with the four-leaf clover method.

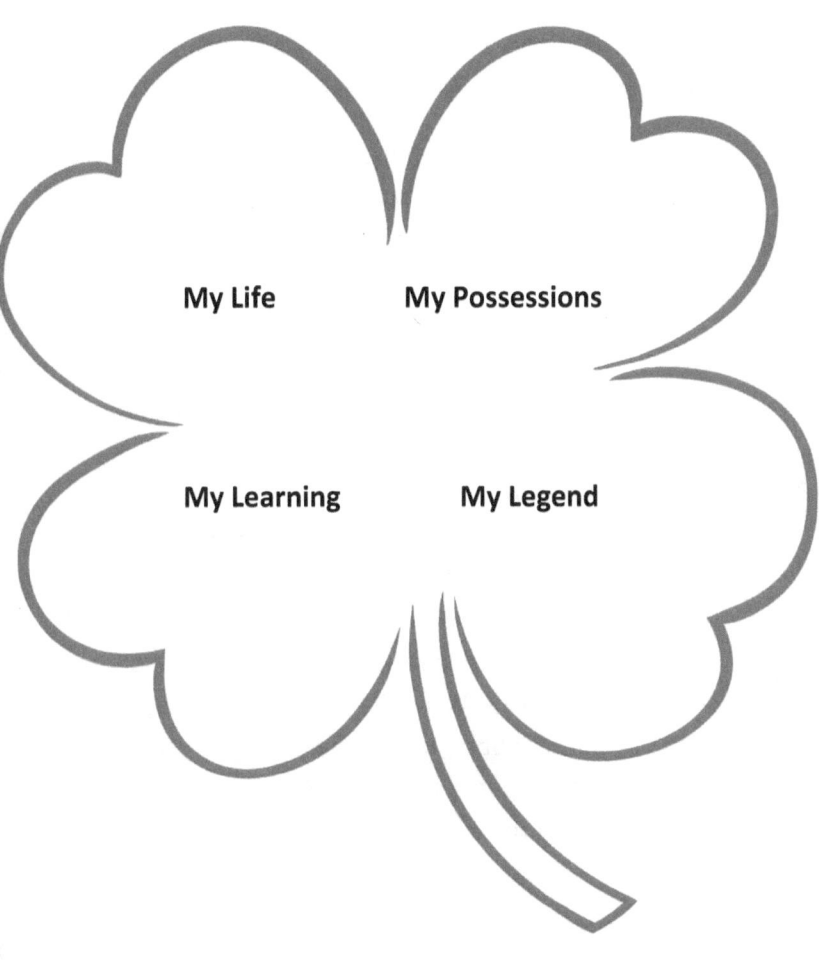

> ➢ Impulse 2 " Four-leaf Clover Method"

Perception exercise: Developing my life vision

The well-known sphere-of-life approach.[4] Many mentors suggest the following four part division as a fixing methodology for better planning of a life vision:

1.   The area of **life/love**: What should my ideal life look like concretely? For the written description, please use, as far as possible, all senses: Sight, hearing, feeling, smell and taste

2.   Area of **property/ownership**: What do I want to own? Which concrete ideas do I have about this?

3.   Area of **learning/competency**: How do I come closer to my personal goal through relevant usable knowledge? A network of knowledge, experiences, new basic beliefs, targeted learning?

4.   Area of **legends/inheritance**: What do we want to leave to this world? What life work? Which legends? What opinions about us? Why do I get up in the morning? Do I have a motive? What motivates me to continue on this path?

---

[4] In particular, derived from the search for the meaning of life

On Area 1 **Life/Love** (Clarity about my being)

What do I see as the meaning of my life? Why am I here? How, concretely, should my ideal life look?

For the written description please use all senses: sight, hearing, feeling, smell and taste

_____

_____

_____

_____

_____

_____

_____

_____

Hint for the exercises: Please use an extra page as needed

What security will I also need in my life in the future? Where and how will I live, in which local environment and with which people? What should my daily routine be in the future?

_____

_____

_____

_____

_____

_____

_____

_____

_____

On Area 2 **Property/Ownership**

What do I want to own? What concrete ideas do I have about this?

How much income do I want to receive in the future – regularly or irregularly?

_____

_____

_____

_____

What kind of income (active or/and passive) do I specifically want to receive in the future?

_____

_____

_____

_____

What assets must I or do I want to have in order to live from the interest on my capital? Do I really want this? What price am I willing to pay in return for what I want to have?

_____

_____

_____

_____

On Area 3 **Learning/Competency**

Now, questions on the fundamental question: What competencies must we acquire, which competencies are needed to come closer to the goal we have set for ourselves. It can be deduced from this what I myself must acquire or learn and what, for instance, I can, delegate.

What abilities and what skills do I need to achieve my goals?

_____

_____

_____

Please determine in writing: on Area 4 **legend/bequest or life's work** – Why or for what do I get up every day?

_____

_____

_____

_____

What motives and reasons and what basic needs do I have, which I want to have fulfilled with the achievement of my vision?

_____

_____

_____

_____

What do I want to achieve personally in the next ten years? What benefits do I provide to other people through this?

_____

_____

_____

_____

_____

_____

_____

Do I want to leave a legend, a life's work after my death and if yes, what?

_____

_____

_____

_____

_____

_____

_____

_____

_____

2nd Milestone – Life Vision

Congratulations!
You have carried out the first step
of the four-leaf clover method
to create your own life vision.

You now know better how you
envision your future life and have set it down in writing.

Keep reviewing, area for area, the quality of your vision, whether this vision represents your ideal dream for your future life.

Are all your wishes also specifically listed?

Hereby, it is also important that your vision of your future affects you emotionally and excites you! Then your life vision will give you the necessary strength to go your own way and to overcome hurdles.

Chapter 3 My personal potential

> ➤ Impulse 3 "My personal abilities"

Do you already *want to* or what *must* you still do?

You already know this. Because your personal success is only possible outside of today's comfort zone, it is urgently necessary that you leave your comfort zone and change into the growth zone as often as possible!

To that end, you must get to know yourself better, so that you can evaluate the behavioral patterns in accordance with which you currently function.

We need a basic structure in our thinking and a comprehensible pattern as a template or as a foundation for our further ways of thinking and our knowledge of ourselves.

Only then can we recognize our own actions and evaluate whether these are suitable or unsuitable for our desired success and only then can this be changed by us voluntarily and purposefully.[5]

For this purpose, your own abilities and skills will, first of all, be brought to the fore and determined.

---

[5] See earlier in the book: Construction levels of personal success

Your approach rests on these abilities and skills and your current values. Moreover, in the next exercise, you first determine which abilities, i.e. talents and which skills you have and make use of.

Do this consciously in order to be able to carry out targeted changes later, should it transpire that certain personal characteristics hinder your desired success, so that you can also consciously use your available abilities.

In the following overview, please first place a check in one checkbox, against your **lived potential,** consisting of abilities (usable talents) and skills (usable learned knowledge) and *afterwards* insert them in the perception exercise that follows in a priority sequence from 1 to 10 with respect to your personal, most important potentials or characteristics.

Perception Exercise on Abilities and Skills

Caption for the exercise: Rank by checking off what applies in either "yes applicable"(left) or rather "no, not applicable". Consequently, the middle circle means neutral, i.e. no determination or knowledge about your own ability or skill. So it means neither "yes" (potential available) nor "no" (potential not available).

Rather yes　O O O O O　rather no

1.	O O O O O	I can speak well
2.	O O O O O	I work creatively
3.	O O O O O	I think conservatively
4.	O O O O O	I think imaginatively
5.	O O O O O	I can explain well
6.	O O O O O	I can negotiate
7.	O O O O O	I can motivate
8.	O O O O O	I can inspire
9.	O O O O O	I can lead well
10.	O O O O O	I can learn well
11.	O O O O O	I am athletic
12.	O O O O O	I can write well
13.	O O O O O	I am good at math
14.	O O O O O	I can read well
15.	O O O O O	I am perceptive
16.	O O O O O	I am disciplined
17.	O O O O O	I am ambitious

18.	O O O O O	I am empathetic
19.	O O O O O	I have charm
20.	O O O O O	I detect opportunities
21.	O O O O O	I recognize time frames
22.	O O O O O	I can plan well
23.	O O O O O	I appreciate beautiful things
24.	O O O O O	I have charisma
25.	O O O O O	I am brave
26.	O O O O O	I am efficient
27.	O O O O O	I have the power of concentration
28.	O O O O O	I am an open person
29.	O O O O O	I am action-oriented
30.	O O O O O	I can express myself well
31.	O O O O O	I am expressive when writing
32.	O O O O O	I can listen well
33.	O O O O O	I am environmentally aware
34.	O O O O O	I can visualize well
35.	O O O O O	I have a positive aura
36.	O O O O O	I think positively
37.	O O O O O	I love myself
38.	O O O O O	I love other people
39.	O O O O O	I am able to form relationships
40.	O O O O O	I believe in myself
41.	O O O O O	I am mentally strong
42.	O O O O O	I have vitality
43.	O O O O O	I am full of energy
44.	O O O O O	I believe in justice
45.	O O O O O	I focus on the goal
46.	O O O O O	I have insight into human nature
47.	O O O O O	I accept myself
48.	O O O O O	I am calm inwardly

49.	O O O O O	I am courageous despite anxiety
50.	O O O O O	I am reliable
51.	O O O O O	I am thankful
52.	O O O O O	I am happy
53.	O O O O O	I am satisfied
54.	O O O O O	I act in a self-rewarding way
55.	O O O O O	I am responsible
56.	O O O O O	I am successful
57.	O O O O O	I am generous
58.	O O O O O	I am constructive
59.	O O O O O	I can let go
60.	O O O O O	I accept the opinions of others
61.	O O O O O	I am consistent
62.	O O O O O	I see problems as opportunities
63.	O O O O O	I see life as a game
64.	O O O O O	I see life as a gift
65.	O O O O O	I see life as a chance
66.	O O O O O	I am mostly in a good mood
67.	O O O O O	I am loyal
68.	O O O O O	I have stamina
69.	O O O O O	I am resourceful
70.	O O O O O	I am a determined person
71.	O O O O O	I am a friendly person
72.	O O O O O	I am amusing
73.	O O O O O	I love adventure
74.	O O O O O	I am a good advisor
75.	O O O O O	I am a good mentor
76.	O O O O O	I am a good coach
77.	O O O O O	I am a good student
78.	O O O O O	I am a patient person
79.	O O O O O	I am trustworthy

80.	O O O O O	I solve problems
81.	O O O O O	I can provide advantages
82.	O O O O O	I have a good education
83.	O O O O O	I am personable
84.	O O O O O	I live in the here and now
85.	O O O O O	I am fond of animals
86.	O O O O O	I am good manually
87.	O O O O O	I have good time management
88.	O O O O O	I can draw well
89.	O O O O O	I can let go easily
90.	O O O O O	I can make repairs well
91.	O O O O O	I can advise well
92.	O O O O O	I can listen well

Here, prepare an add-on list of your other abilities, skills and positive qualities, which were not mentioned in the list:

_____

_____

_____

_____

_____

_____

_____

_____

_____

Now please make a note of your ten most important abilities (talents) and skills (competencies) in what you think is the right sequence:

1

_____

2

_____

3

_____

4

_____

5

_____

6

_____

7

_____

8

_____

9

_____

10

_____

3rd Milestone – Abilities & Skills

Congratulations!

Now you are aware of your main abilities and skills and have arranged them in some kind of order.

But now, there is still something else to do!

Ask the people in your living environment to share with you, from their perspective, what your main talents are:

The first three abilities that occur to them are sufficient. Often you may not be aware of them, but you also have these talents.

Please also record these talents and consciously utilize them in the future.

Recorded feedback results from third parties about my previously unknown talents.

_____

_____

Now, after you have organized your abilities and skills and have them available, further questions on their manifestation:

In your opinion, which abilities and skills have you used with your most significant life successes?

_____

_____

_____

_____

_____

_____

_____

_____

In your opinion, which abilities and skills do you have that are unique (different from others = DFO)

_____

_____

_____

_____

_____

_____

_____

_____

➢ Impulse 4 "The obituary you wish for"

Now we come to the next exercise. Basically, this is a self-discovery exercise. With this exercise, we imagine that various people are bidding us farewell (for example when you are 99 years old)

These can be our partners, children, friends, acquaintances, relatives, colleagues or people in the public sphere, whereby we imagine what we would wish, what they would say about us at our grave during our burial.

Who should be at our grave?

What would we want to hear from others about ourselves?

How do I want to be seen by others?

What kind of person do I want to develop into?

In my opinion, who should I be in the future?

I scrutinize all that with this self-discovery exercise. This exercise also helps us with our decisions because we can achieve clarity about our goals and thinking in this way.

In particular, I know from this how I should behave in future actions in order to become this person, whom I imagine myself to be in the future graveside-speech situation.

Hereby, this has to do with my own **guiding principle** and improving the life vision I have already prepared and discovering more about myself.

Among other things, I recognize through this exercise, what kind of person I want to be. Thus, this person is, for me, the optimized person of the one I am today. In the future, this person will live my goals and, in the course of my life, I will develop into this ideal figure. So, the way determines the goal, because my personality development is paramount for this. This is necessary so that I can become the personality that my future life content (which I already defined in the first four-leaf clover life area exercise) can, then, also live. This gives me the ability to further develop myself in order to also actually be able to take on this position in the future. This person is mostly not identical with the person that I am currently.

This person has other character traits and other competencies than you already have today! This person has further developed in the desired direction you wish, which you also manifest further and more concretely with this exercise. Thus you find a further fine adjustment in relation to your life vision. You can, therefore, proceed in an even more focused way and more finely tune your strategy for action.

Also, with this exercise, the written manifestation of your thought related to your wishes concerning your person is of great importance. Touch upon each person who is saying good-bye and write a talk for each person, which will be held at your grave. Just as you imagine, in the way that would, in your opinion. be optimal . Begin the talk simply with key words and the character traits you would want to hear about, who says this about you and what behaviors were repeated

Person:

_____

Talk:

_____

_____

Person:

Talk:

Person:

_____

Talk:

_____

_____

_____

_____

_____

_____

_____

_____

_____

Person:

_____

Talk:

_____

_____

_____

_____

_____

_____

_____

_____

_____

4th Milestone - Obituary

Effect of the obituary you wrote:

If you took sufficient time to write your obituary, you will note how revealing it was to engage with it. Now you can draw conclusions on what really matters to you.

Your important life vision and your goals are now clearer.
You feel better organized and focused.
You feel your intuition.
Your direction is now visible and tangible!

Some notes concerning the effect[6] and the discoveries from the exercise:

_____

_____

_____

_____

_____

_____

_____

_____

---

[6] Which ideal image do I have of myself in the future, how and whom will I become?

Chapter 4 My individual values

If we wanted to define the term "values", we could understand values or ideals as those that are characteristics or qualities, which a person considers desirable for himself or a third party. These values are the basis on which we make our decisions and which contribute to how we organize our actions.

What is really important for you and why? Our values reveal a great deal. Over the course of our life, we have acquired values, be it through our upbringing, through our environment or through other factors in our lives. That also means that we can change our values at any time. This is, then, particularly important if our present values have prevented us from achieving our goals. This, is also considered under the aspect that our values strongly influence our way of thinking, our perspective on things and, ultimately, our actions.

Through the knowledge and the deliberate and conscious shaping of your own decision criteria – here, your values - you can consciously regain your own control over your life journey. This is important due in particular to the fact that our own values must correspond with our goals if we also want to achieve them.

A conflict between your values and your goals should be cleared up because otherwise, you cannot achieve your goals. You yourself will always stand in the way.

With the help of the next exercise, you will be in a position to determine your real values and, consequently, after this exercise, you will be able to change your values, little by little, so that you can develop other behaviors and, thereby, develop a promising *modus operandi*[7].

Perception exercise: Developing my personal values

What is important to me in my vision, in particular, which values?

Exercise description for the development of your personal order of values:

The following task consists first of your seeking some individually applicable values from a list of selected and recommended values

Subsequently, add your own individual values not available on the list.

Later, prepare a priority list, i.e. you now set the TOP-TEN values in a sequence running from 1 to 10 on your value scale, according to your estimation of their importance.

Thereby, you emphasize the leading values for you as a person, in accordance with which, among other things, unconsciously influenced decisions occur in daily life

---

[7] Lat.: „The Art of Action" describes a Latin phrase which refers to the manner of action by a person.

In the further course of things, this compiled value scale, now visible, serves to enable necessary course corrections if present values do not fit with your actual vision or would hinder its fulfillment.

➢ Impulse 5 "My personal value system"

What values are important for me?

In this exercise, first give thought to YOUR values and arrange these in accordance with your ideas. In a second step, you will arrange them by writing them in a table in accordance with priorities 1 to 10 in your personal sequence

Approach:

1. First, please arrange your individual values from the predefined list and check them off.

2. Afterwards, select your "TOP-TEN" values from the predefined list, by bringing these 10 individual values in the right order (for you) in the table prepared for you.

List for ascertaining values

Which values do I live out?

Which values do I treasure?

Which values are important to me?

Which values influence my actions every day?

Please follow up by checking off the appropriate predefined value in this exercise, mentioned above, to determine your overall values:

Exercise caption: Arrange by ticking appropriately in either:

rather "yes" O O O O O rather "no"

1.	O O O O O	Change
2.	O O O O O	Adventure
3.	O O O O O	Mindfulness
4.	O O O O O	Attention
5.	O O O O O	Agility
6.	O O O O O	Sincerity
7.	O O O O O	Activity
8.	O O O O O	Actuality
9.	O O O O O	Acceptance
10.	O O O O O	Appreciation
11.	O O O O O	Differentness
12.	O O O O O	Grace
13.	O O O O O	Respect
14.	O O O O O	Decency
15.	O O O O O	Aesthetic
16.	O O O O O	Openness
17.	O O O O O	Attentiveness
18.	O O O O O	Tranquility
19.	O O O O O	Equilibrium
20.	O O O O O	Authenticity
21.	O O O O O	Balance
22.	O O O O O	Enthusiasm
23.	O O O O O	Cautiousness
24.	O O O O O	Persistence
25.	O O O O O	Relationships
26.	O O O O O	Modesty
27.	O O O O O	Prudence
28.	O O O O O	Charisma

29.	O O O O O	Education
30.	O O O O O	Reliability
31.	O O O O O	Strong Character
32.	O O O O O	Resilience
33.	O O O O O	Thankfulness
34.	O O O O O	Humility
35.	O O O O O	Discipline
36.	O O O O O	Being the Best
37.	O O O O O	Self-reliance
38.	O O O O O	Effectiveness
39.	O O O O O	Ambition
40.	O O O O O	Enthusiasm
41.	O O O O O	Sensitivity
42.	O O O O O	Efficiency
43.	O O O O O	Honesty
44.	O O O O O	Relaxation
45.	O O O O O	Decisiveness
46.	O O O O O	Honor
47.	O O O O O	Empathy
48.	O O O O O	Decisiveness
49.	O O O O O	Excellence
50.	O O O O O	Fairness
51.	O O O O O	Focused
52.	O O O O O	Fitness
53.	O O O O O	Family
54.	O O O O O	Diligence
55.	O O O O O	Flexibility
56.	O O O O O	Freedom
57.	O O O O O	Financial Freedom
58.	O O O O O	Joy
59.	O O O O O	Friendship

60.	O O O O O	Friendliness
61.	O O O O O	Peace
62.	O O O O O	Cheerfulness
63.	O O O O O	Solicitousness
64.	O O O O O	Wealth
65.	O O O O O	Patience
66.	O O O O O	Belief
67.	O O O O O	Geographical freedom
68.	O O O O O	Money
69.	O O O O O	Enjoyment
70.	O O O O O	Luck
71.	O O O O O	Camaraderie
72.	O O O O O	Calmness
73.	O O O O O	Conviviality
74.	O O O O O	Fairness
75.	O O O O O	Feeling of security
76.	O O O O O	Health
77.	O O O O O	Sociality
78.	O O O O O	Trustworthiness
79.	O O O O O	Generosity
80.	O O O O O	Kindness
81.	O O O O O	Harmony
82.	O O O O O	Tenacity
83.	O O O O O	Helpfulness
84.	O O O O O	Dedication
85.	O O O O O	Hopeful
86.	O O O O O	Civility
87.	O O O O O	Humor
88.	O O O O O	Challenge
89.	O O O O O	Idealism
90.	O O O O O	Innovation

91.	O O O O O	inspiring
92.	O O O O O	Individualism
93.	O O O O O	Integrity
94.	O O O O O	Intelligent
95.	O O O O O	Interest
96.	O O O O O	Intuition
97.	O O O O O	Wisdom
98.	O O O O O	Artistry
99.	O O O O O	Physical Fitness
100.	O O O O O	Wants children
101.	O O O O O	Conservative
102.	O O O O O	Cultivated
103.	O O O O O	Monitoring
104.	O O O O O	Creativity
105.	O O O O O	Career
106.	O O O O O	Laughter
107.	O O O O O	Passion
108.	O O O O O	Service
109.	O O O O O	Nonchalance
110.	O O O O O	Logic
111.	O O O O O	Vitality
112.	O O O O O	Joy in living
113.	O O O O O	Zest for life
114.	O O O O O	Kindness
115.	O O O O O	Loyalty
116.	O O O O O	Sympathy
117.	O O O O O	Power
118.	O O O O O	motivating
119.	O O O O O	Boldness
120.	O O O O O	Humanity
121.	O O O O O	Sustainability

122.	O O O O O	Altruism
123.	O O O O O	Neutrality
124.	O O O O O	Openness
125.	O O O O O	Optimism
126.	O O O O O	Orderly
127.	O O O O O	Sense of order
128.	O O O O O	Organizational talent
129.	O O O O O	Conscientiousness
130.	O O O O O	Pragmatism
131.	O O O O O	Fantasy
132.	O O O O O	Punctuality
133.	O O O O O	Personality
134.	O O O O O	Personal Growth
135.	O O O O O	Professionality
136.	O O O O O	Pragmatic
137.	O O O O O	Presence
138.	O O O O O	Punctuality
139.	O O O O O	Realism
140.	O O O O O	Fidelity
141.	O O O O O	Reflection
142.	O O O O O	Respect
143.	O O O O O	Purity
144.	O O O O O	Religion
145.	O O O O O	Prosperity
146.	O O O O O	Fame
147.	O O O O O	Reputation
148.	O O O O O	Consideration
149.	O O O O O	Placid nature
150.	O O O O O	Astuteness
151.	O O O O O	Sensuousness
152.	O O O O O	Spontaneity

153.	O O O O O	Cleanliness
154.	O O O O O	Self-discipline
155.	O O O O O	Self-assurance
156.	O O O O O	Self-control
157.	O O O O O	Self-confidence
158.	O O O O O	Self-reliance
159.	O O O O O	Self-esteem
160.	O O O O O	Sexuality
161.	O O O O O	Sensitive
162.	O O O O O	Safety
163.	O O O O O	Solidarity
164.	O O O O O	Diligence
165.	O O O O O	Status
166.	O O O O O	Spirituality
167.	O O O O O	Thriftiness
168.	O O O O O	Pleasure
169.	O O O O O	Steadfastness
170.	O O O O O	Quick-wittedness
171.	O O O O O	Sympathy
172.	O O O O O	Fulfillment of duties
173.	O O O O O	Team spirit
174.	O O O O O	Fortitude
175.	O O O O O	Sharing
176.	O O O O O	Tolerance
177.	O O O O O	Traditional
178.	O O O O O	Transparency
179.	O O O O O	Loyalty
180.	O O O O O	Proficiency
181.	O O O O O	Conviction
182.	O O O O O	Impartial
183.	O O O O O	Incorruptibility

184.	O O O O O	Responsibility
185.	O O O O O	Diversity
186.	O O O O O	Setting an example
187.	O O O O O	Dependability
188.	O O O O O	Trust
189.	O O O O O	Forgiveness
190.	O O O O O	Vigilance
191.	O O O O O	Appreciation
192.	O O O O O	Further development
193.	O O O O O	Wisdom
194.	O O O O O	Competition
195.	O O O O O	Truth
196.	O O O O O	Will power
197.	O O O O O	Foresightedness
198.	O O O O O	Affluence
199.	O O O O O	Dignity
200.	O O O O O	Determination
201.	O O O O O	Tenderness
202.	O O O O O	Time latitude
203.	O O O O O	Trustworthiness
204.	O O O O O	Expediency
205.	O O O O O	Belonging
206.	O O O O O	Affinity
207.	O O O O O	Confidence
208.	O O O O O	Goals
209.	O O O O O	Satisfaction

Do you recognize values that are not mentioned here?
Please note them too!

_____

_____

_____

_____

_____

_____

_____

_____

_____

_____

MY TOP-TEN-VALUES! Now please arrange your values in the correct sequence (1-10)

1
_____

2
_____

3
_____

4
_____

5
_____

6

_____

7

_____

8

_____

9

_____

10

_____

_____

5th Milestone - Values

Super! You have reached the next milestone!

You have now set your TOP-TEN value scale and now know the values in accordance with which you orient your actions.

When we change our values, we also change our entire action and behavioral pattern.

In other words, we draw other people into our life.

> Impulse 6 "Individual Potential Analysis"

The personal, individual calling

Significant for defining your own calling is having determined your own values. Discovering your talents and honoring your personal motivation certainly make up one of the greatest intrinsic motivators in our life. Therefore, it is important that we first work out a potential analysis with our strengths and weaknesses, so that we pinpoint that which does not give us pleasure and what our true strengths are. Real strengths are always enjoyable and will sustainably motivate us for important tasks

The SWOT analysis is composed of the following abbreviations from four English terms:

Strengths vs. **W**eaknesses

Opportunities vs. **T**hreats .

The strengths and weaknesses concern the internal analysis, hence the questions about one's own self, while the opportunities and risks focus on the external analysis, hence the questions about the circumstances, the environment.

Area 1 Strengths/Opportunities

The mixture of strengths and opportunities results in the question of which opportunities result from which strengths. These strengths should be developed. Appropriate measures should lead to action.

Area 2 Strengths/Risks

With the mixture of strengths and risks, the question arises of which strengths can minimize which risks. These strengths should be **safeguarded** and appropriate measures should lead to action.

Area 3 Weaknesses/opportunities

With the mixture of weaknesses and opportunities, the question arises of which weaknesses can be eliminated in order to be able to use new opportunities. These weaknesses should be **made up for** and appropriate measures should lead to action.

Area 4 Weaknesses/Risks

With the mixture of weaknesses and risks, the question arises of which weaknesses can lead to risks, in order to determine appropriate defensive strategies. These risks should be **removed** and appropriate measures should lead to action. Now create your own SWOT analysis by recording your strengths, then compare the external circumstances in the form of opportunities and risks and then determine the action required.

Also, please compare your opportunities and risks in order to create the concrete action required for this.

Try to develop as many areas as possible with the SWOT-analysis because, in this way, you can influence your intrinsic motivators.

Make sure that you align the strengths that you worked out with your vision. Check the extent to which this can be utilized for your vision and how this can bring you closer to your goal. Please make this comparison in the following Chapter 5, "My Personal Mission", because you can use your strengths for the benefit of others and should be able to achieve the personal success you desire.

Now, enjoy exploring your possibilities by using the SWOT analysis.

An example:

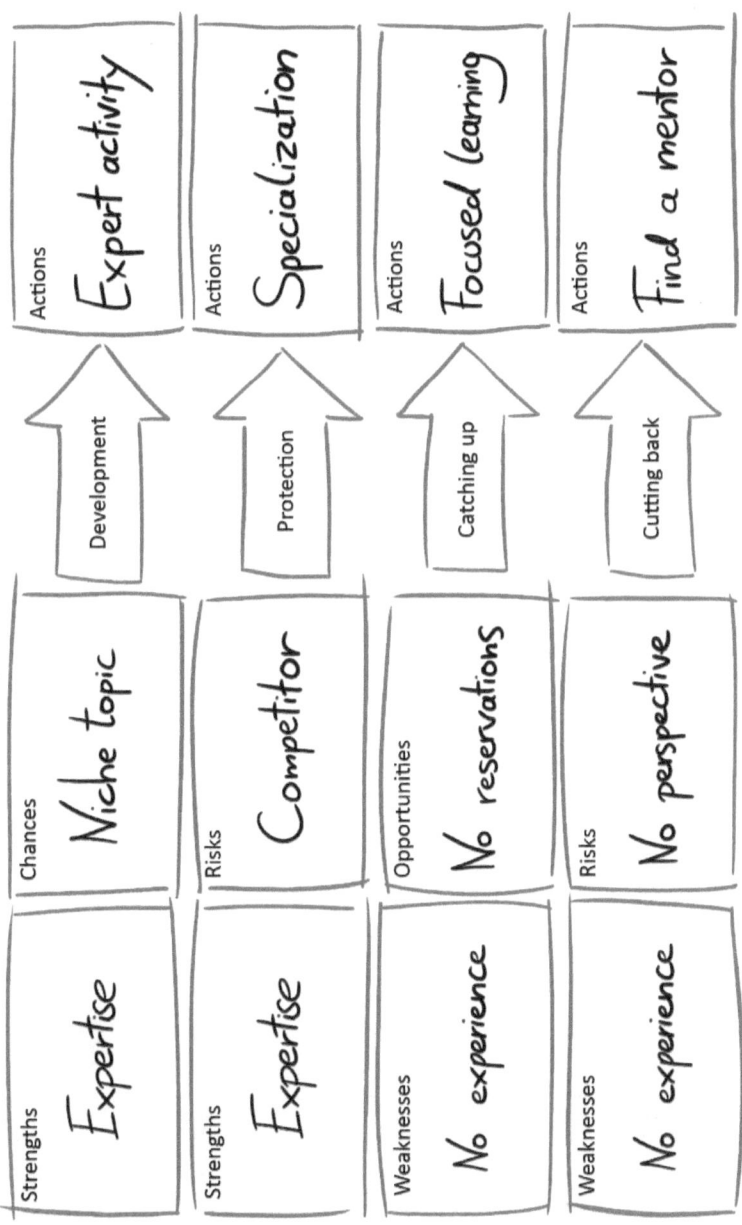

Now create your own personal SWOT-Analysis

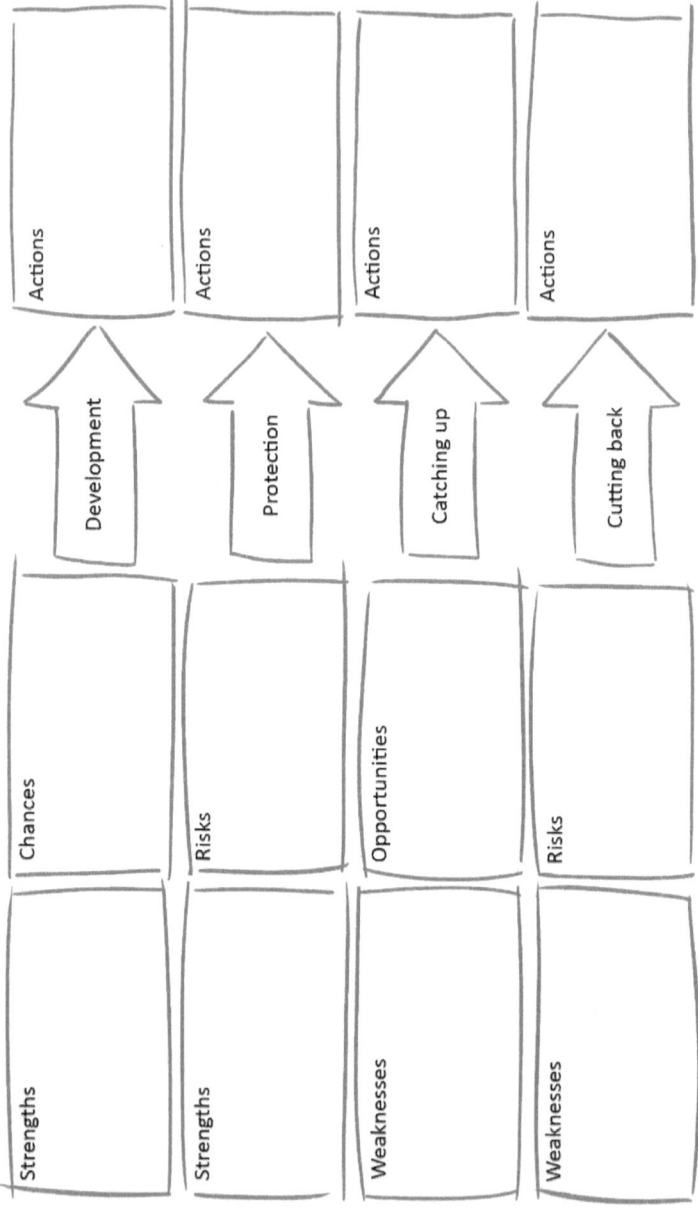

6th Milestone - SWOT-Analysis

Super! Now you have also

developed the next milestone

and currently recognize your

personal motivation since you

have made clear your motivation, since you

have highlighted your most important motivators[8] via the

SWOT analysis.

In the future, only pursue your strengths and delegate the rest!

---

[8] Your own motivational factors (which are self-perpetuating)

Chapter 5 My personal mission

Perception exercise: Explore *your possible value for others due to your talents.*

What benefits do you produce for other people by making optimal use of your talents?

_____

_____

_____

_____

_____

_____

_____

Who, in particular which people have **which advantage** due to your path and your mission?

_____

_____

_____

_____

_____

_____

_____

_____

_____

_____

When, at what point, do these people obtain and make use of this advantage?

_____

_____

_____

_____

_____

How and in what way can other people ultimately obtain this benefit?

_____

_____

_____

_____

_____

How much effort must these people make or which road must these people take to receive this benefit?

_____

_____

_____

_____

_____

What can I offer that justifies the trade-off or, even better, exceeds it?

_____

_____

_____

_____

_____

7th. Milestone - Mission

Think about the usefulness instead
of the profit!
Now think about what
you can do for your counterpart,
for example, your fellow human beings!
Here, the usefulness for your fellow
human beings, not "what can I sell them?"
should be paramount

Thus, no thought of profit should be in the foreground, but rather the usefulness for our fellow human beings. Your question is:

What different or increased service does my fellow human being get from me?

Motto: It is more blessed to give than to receive for:

"Only he who gives much, will receive much"

Chapter 6 My personal basic beliefs

The famous American manager, Henry Ford once summed it up:

> **"Whether you believe you can do it or whether you believe you cannot do it, you will, in any case, be proved correct."**

The substance of this citation is, first of all, what we think about ourselves and the world, will become true for us.

Hence, we have once again arrived in the world of thoughts. Everything that we can actively imagine, that we accept as our opinion and attitude, so that this becomes our belief, means that we ourselves create our own perception of the world. In other words, that which we think, will also create our future.

What, then, are basic beliefs? We know that basic beliefs influence our actions, our kind of approach. Basic beliefs arise as we are growing up through our appraisal, through our own experience and that of others, and the formation of adult opinions, which grow out of this.

This formation of opinion leads to conviction, to our strengthened attitude towards those things which we internalize and which become our beliefs. These beliefs, i.e., our perception of the world, ultimately determine our own day-to-day perception and our actions and the perception in our memories.

Our thought processes are formed by our basic beliefs and also by the frequency with which we reside in which level of thinking with our day-to-day thoughts.

It is, therefore, necessary to recognize our own basic beliefs in order to be able to bring about changes in our day-to-day actions. Only in this way, is promising self-guidance possible, overriding old unusable basic beliefs and making new purposeful basic beliefs implementable.

I can only implement my vision successfully, only go my own way successfully, if my subconscious, where my basic beliefs are programmed, provides supportive and positive basic beliefs to promote my successful way.

Implicitly, this means that limiting or blocking basic beliefs can hinder us from achieving our personal wishes and goals.

Thereby, it is clear that if we change our thoughts and our previous negative belief structure, not much stands in the way of our personal life visions. Because we can use the supportive power of the subconscious to achieve our goals!

8th Milestone – Basic Beliefs

What is inside is outside too!
Your basic beliefs create either
positive thought impulses or
negative thought impulses!

Positive thought impulses are advantageous because they lead more quickly to a decision.

Negative thought impulses don't bring you further but, rather, these block you with regard to your will and your goals

Thus, you must discover your actual basic beliefs in order to replace them with usable basic beliefs.

Chapter 7 My behavioral Change

When you reflect on it, it is alleged that change is the only constant in the universe! This may be so. Basically, we change ourselves every minute of our lives. Also, we are currently in an era in which we are confronted with a great many changes on different levels, which also come our way in our environment and for which we must prepare ourselves.

Einstein once said that we cannot solve problems on the same thought level on which the problem emerges today. In order that we can make use of and implement these new challenges positively and successfully, we must prepare ourselves for these challenges consistently and systematically with another way of thinking.

Thus, it is enormously important, especially for personality development and individual self-optimization, that we reflect on ourselves. This is in order to recognize the approaches to understanding our own way of working and, in particular, to recognize our previous habits.

Therefore, it is, first of all, advisable to reflect on our behavioral perspective. Only in this way, can we more easily understand how and why our "inner sloth" can so easily and so often defeat us.

Furthermore, this is important so that we can position ourselves, simply because it is possible through our intrinsic motivation to conquer our inner sloth, at least temporarily.

Overcome your inner sloth with behavioral changes

Then, in order to be able bring about sustainable success, a method must be developed, which makes us winners through a system or with a new habit.

Hereby it is important to consider that the intrinsic motivation and with that, our will stands at the beginning of a planned behavioral change, which should, in time, be replaced with a habit. This is so we can generate sustainable success. Through the momentum[9] of a new habit, which we have created, we will be in the position that our "inner sloth" must not always be defeated through our will. So we can have phases in which we can overcome our doubts about our ability through our new habit, the desired behavioral change.

Implementation systems for the desired change can also lead to success. But let's first deal with the next impulse, the area of planned individual behavioral change.

---

[9] Here, what is meant in this connection is that, when I have once set something in motion, it needs less energy to keep it in motion than it would need if I had to set it in motion repeatedly

> ➤ Impulse 7 "Behavioral Change"

Changing my personality first means clarity in thinking

For a start, it is important to bring about clarity in thinking. In the first place. First of all, something in our personality development to successful people, aims – not without good reason – at our achieving clarity.

Clarity about our WHY, clarity about our basic beliefs and values as well as clarity about our interim goals for our individual success!

Moreover, with respect to our path, we must also have clarity about the service to be rendered on our side, as well as about our future networks, and also about what price, in the form of a sacrifice, we are willing to make for what goal and whether we are prepared to provide the required trade-off.

Clarity puts us in the position to implement necessary path corrections or even goal corrections. Through this, we can occupy ourselves on our way with the HOW and, consequently, with the necessary subject matter of the action!

Let's look again more closely at the individual phases to better understand this.

These phases help with **recognition** of the measures with which we can best help ourselves in the individual phases described and how, in these phases, we can actively use the situation for our success.

How does the situation look and what possibilities for successfully managing it are available to me:

Phase 1: Current-State of the Situation: My situation is not satisfactory!

Recommended measure: Success building-block action, i.e. you should initiate something, take action, briefly: **Do.** Don't delay too long but act – in the worst case it will be an experience!   Winners never lose because they either accumulate further experience on the way to their personal goal or win immediately!

This is the only perspective or mindset that leads us to success. You must seek out the right way to your personal vision!

Successful people often use the 72-hour or 3-day-rule for this. This means, that when we want to change something, we should begin with it in a space from right now to 72 hours after our decision. Otherwise, there is the risk that we will postpone it until forever and a day.

Phase 2: Your desired situation: My outcome should be improved!

Recommended Measure: Success-building block technique, i.e, you should use another technique! You are already doing this with the implementation exercise in this workbook! You build on your personality structure by using techniques that you have not yet used. With the sequence of using the exercises, you construct another more successful technique in dealing with your perception, your thought and your own personality. Furthermore, you change your perspective on the things in our world. Your awareness and your perception change.

Phase 3: Your desired situation: I want to have recognition and natural authority, natural assertiveness and charismsa!

Recommended Measures: Success-building block personality development or, more exactly, conscious personality development as a success factor. **Leave your comfort zone as often as possible and change to the growth zone.** It is only there that growth is possible and this only happens by battling against the inner, painful feelings and overcoming them.

For these small and large victories over your present practices, allow your personality to grow little by little. Thereby, your potential unfolds. Become aware of your potential!

Phase 4: Your desired situation: I want to lead a happy and contented life

Recommended Measures: An expanded world view, replace obstructive messages and exchange them for uplifting messages.

This can only succeed through another conscious vision of things and through intense observation of ourselves. Here too, it can be beneficial to be able to distinguish the *important* from the *urgent* in your goal and your vision.

Note: Together, we will develop the topical area of mission, fundamental beliefs and the precision adjustment of the four-leaf clover method in another chapter, which follows

Phase 5: Your desired situation: I want to design my own future myself

Recommended measure: Be the designer of your own future through visualization of your own desired, possible future. Here, a new view must be developed with respect to your own person, also, in particular, to a clearly defined life vision of your own. This produces the big picture of your possible future. Here also, the question arises of which person will live your life in the future. Who must I be in order to live this desired life? What kind of personality? How must I develop myself so that I can live the life I want for the future? What kind of personality? What must I do to arrive there? Here, it can be necessary to be aware of your goals and your vision in order to differentiate the *important* from the *urgent* and be able to derive clarity in thinking.

My life vision, which I want to develop for myself, should be very concrete, so concrete as possible. Here, all senses should be used in visualizing my future. I should be able to imagine what positive feelings are involved in my future.

Furthermore, partial goals, so-called "milestones", should then be derived from my vision. In this way, I can prepare myself for my life vision with a perspective of, for example, ten years, step by step, originating from the goal over years, months and weeks until the present day. So, in the best case, I will know every day what needs to be done in order to achieve the large goal, step by step, as in the example of my life vision, in ten years.

Furthermore, regarding my own time management, I have constructed a compass planning instead of an hour planning, which means I approach my goal as planned, step by step. With mere time planning, this does not happen! Here, the focus on my life vision is lacking.

Everyone knows the method in high performance sports, which, through the power of imagination, leads more quickly from the target vision to achieving that vision. Whoever develops attractive and concrete visions of the future is supported by this mental fixation of the subconscious on achieving greater visions as well as the short-term and, in particular, the long-term goals! With a lack of orientation and with obstacles along the way, this also helps us not to lose sight of the objective!

Through this look at the various structuring levels, you should be made aware of the fact that this represents the basis for a behavioral change since, in each of these levels, wherever you discover a problem, you can step in and consciously bring about changes relating to your personality.

After you recognize, via the following self-reflection exercise, the extent to which you have been influenced by your basic beliefs in your life up until now and what decisions were made as a result, it is now important to deal with your own motivation.

For this reason in particular, we must determine and recognize what we want and which of our beliefs and attitudes seem to be credible and, thereby, feasible to implement. How, therefore can you support **your** will?

Now, let's summarize the topical area of desire or our own will:

We must assume responsibility for ourselves!

Whoever assumes responsibiity, should always act only for his own reasons, only with his own free will! Reasons determined by outside forces should not play any role in this.

Only a person's own way leads to success.

Hereby, it is your own goal setting, your own vision, which differentiates between victory or failure. How do I now systematically develop a strong will? On this topic, let's look next at some important parameters and steps with which I can strengthen my own motivation and support my will.

Perception Exercise: Reflecting on behavioral perspectives

1.Basic assessment: Our own experiences or those of others first shape our opinions, then our inner attitudes and personal perceptions of things and, finally, our basic beliefs, since we "believe" that the world is the way we "see" it and, therefore, we assess how it apparently represents us!

Now think calmly and please reflect here on some examples from your life:

_____

_____

_____

_____

_____

_____

_____

2. Basic assessment: The evaluation of our experiences is individual. This evaluation results from our view of the things that were based upon the experience we have had up until now and our self-assessment of this experience.

Now think calmly and please reflect here on some examples from your life:

_____

_____

_____

_____

_____

_____

_____

_____

3. Question on this: What negative and positive basic beliefs have which influence on our thinking?

Consider this calmly and please reflect here on some examples from your life:

_____

_____

_____

_____

_____

_____

_____

_____

4. Fundamental determination

Our subconscious reacts on the basis of our previous experiences, which we have had over the course of our life to date, be this through transfer of knowledge and experiences, which were provided by our environment, or through experiences that we had or created ourselves as well as through the evaluation of our life events or life circumstances. Our subconscious implements our decisions from our consciousness without asking about them, works permanently and parallel with the basic beliefs programmed in our subconscious!

Consider this calmly and please reflect here with some examples from your life:

_____

_____

_____

_____

_____

9th Milestone – Behavioral change

Behavioral change is an everlasting Process!

We now know that, with a planned change of behavior, our will is only the start in order to get it going.
However, with time it should be replaced by a habit.

And we have asked questions on self-reflection in order to be able to adopt new habits, so that we can be consciously in accord with our vision.

Chapter 8 Finale with Success Pitch

> *"If you do not have a life vision, which you long for and towards which you are working, which you want to achieve with all your strength, then it is possible that there is also no motive for you to work hard."*
>
> *Erich Fromm*

Fine adjustment and summary of the four-leaf clover method for the success pitch.

Definition of success pitch: Success pitch was derived from the American term "Elevator Pitch":

Elevator Pitch stands for a method in which a brief summary of an idea is presented within a short timeframe, such as, for example, during an elevator ride. Hereby, the chosen conversation partner is convinced of the value of an idea.

The success pitch derived from it (in German) stands for a short description concerning your ideas vis-à-vis a third party (or you practice alone at home in front of a mirror), here with respect to your presentation about your personality and your mission.

From now on, your changed view of things, thanks to the knowledge from the previous exercises, should expand and improve the first draft of your vision which you prepared in the framework of four-leaf clover method. This will now be more specific because you have become more aware of yourself. Now you know who you are and where you want to go.

The following fine adjustment of the four-leaf clover method for the success-pitch means that you must develop **a commitment to your future** and, at the same time, prepare your success-pitch

This is based on your previously prepared 4-leaf clover method, which you will now refine again and be able to make your life vision even more concrete.

Now, please finalize your results from the impulse exercise, by completing the following four-leaf clover exercises and then, please briefly put it in writing:

*1 Four-leaf clover method - Life Area: **Live/Love**, my future life environment (People, places, daily routine, etc.).*

_____

_____

_____

_____

_____

_____

_____

_____

_____

_____

Dr. Norbert Hermann

*2. Four-leaf clover method – Life Area: **Possessions/What I own**; my future possessions (real estate, bank balance, things, etc.)*

_____

_____

_____

_____

_____

_____

_____

_____

_____

_____

_____

_____

_____

_____

_____

_____

_____

_____

_____

_____

3 Four-leaf clover method – Life Area:
Learning/Competence
What knowledge must I acquire primarily to achieve my vision? What do I want to know about this? What burning interests do I have?

---

4 Four-leaf clover method – Life Area:
Legends/Inheritance

What do I want to pass on, what benefit for third parties? What do I want to create which also remains after my death?

_____

_____

_____

_____

_____

_____

_____

_____

➢ Impulse 8 "My individual success pitch"

Perception Exercise: My Success Pitch

The Success Pitch should be short (30 seconds to 3 minutes) and concise.

Here, please stick to the following sequence when developing your success statement:

First the guidelines for the **approach**:

1. Attract attention
2. Awaken interest
3. Trigger demand
4. Evoke action

The following **content** should be incorporated into your success pitch:

Who are you?

What can you do?

What benefit do you provide for other people?

What do you want?

What should your counterpart/fellow human being do now? How can you help your counterpart/fellow human being further?

My personal success pitch:

_____

_____

_____

_____

_____

_____

_____

_____

_____

_____

_____

_____

_____

_____

_____

_____

_____

_____

_____

_____

_____

_____

_____

_____

_____

_____

_____

Now you can introduce the success pitch to a third party stranger, briefly and memorably.

With this, you commit yourself to your life vision. Please do this repeatedly in writing without fail! Thereby, you will remain on the right course. Commit yourself concretely to yourself!

Check at regular intervals whether your desired direction is correct.

Keep in mind that, by writing, you are already programming your subconscious with this commitment intellectually in the direction of your goal.

10th Final Milestone!

Congratulations! You have a

reason to celebrate!

You have succeeded and determined your personality structure.

Thereby, you have achieved your primary goal with this book.

Now you know exactly which abilities and skills you have. Along with this, you also know which activities you will delegate in the future.

You know your vision and your successful future will, thus, be predictable and visible.

You know your mission and now know the benefits with which you can enrich others.

You know your value and, through targeted modifications, you can change your course of action

In presentation situations, you immediately have your success pitch, your success statement, present.

You have gained clarity about your future and orientation.

You are now ready to consciously promote your personality growth with a system!

Chapter ON TOP – Growth through Implementation

A selection of fundamental relevant growth tips and turbos for our areas in personality development:

Growth driver 1: Mentor and Network

Basically, a mentor tries to encourage the mentee in his personal and cognitive development and in releasing his potential

A mentor is viewed as a good and capable mentor when he himself has already had achievements in the area in which the mentee still wants to achieve. The mentor outlines requirements and provides encouragement for his mentee

Also, the mentor will always only influence his mentee positively, so that he can also discover his potential and, ultimately, fully develop it.

In order to grow optimally, it makes sense to utilize the mentor's expertise.

Often, mentors become aware of us through our good services and through our attitude. They recognize our eligibility from our actions, which reflect our abilities and so recognize the skill sets which would be worth considering!

Looking at it another way, we ourselves should always recognize someone as a mentor who represents a role model for us and whose words rest upon his own experience. He should already have achieved and experienced what I want to achieve – or many times over that!

One of my mentors once said that the mentor, with his achievements and his successes, should even go well beyond my current goal focus, so that we achieve more than that for which we currently have confidence or can imagine.

However you can also find mentors through the founding or the expansion of a business network because, in a good network, you will always find those who are experts in your particular area.

Incidentally, it will always be the case that a mentor is a person who behaves like someone who actually wants to promote your talents.

That means that you can always recognize your mentor from his deeds. No one should ask anyone whether he would like to be his mentor. A mentor will always only support those in whom he also sees relevant talents, which he would gladly promote.

What matters here is recognizing, in good time, this behavioral sign in a potential promoter and then building the desired relationship of trust to his mentor, consciously and correctly

Always keep in mind that a mentor wants to give something, wants to experience joy in mentoring, but without pressure!

However, don't confuse a mentor with a coach! A coach is your temporary limited supporter, whereby the relationship mostly rests on a business footing.

By contrast, a mentor often means a long-term relationship, which is based both on the business, in particular, a functioning one, but also only on a very personal level. This means that the mentor also holds up a mirror for you and quite consciously poses critical questions.

Due to his personality structure, it would be completely clear to an experienced mentor that only through the process of reflection could he effect further development in the mentee.

Consequently, it must be clear to the mentee from the outset, that he must also deal with the mentor's criticism because only through this process can the desired further development towards the personal goals be optimally brought about.

Hereby, the mentor functions as an event- and effect accelerator with respect to your binding, declared vision and to the required personality development for this, since you will be inspired by him and, in difficult situations and when making difficult decision,s you can profit from his experience

Important! Thank and inform your mentor when you make use of the practical knowledge of your mentor for yourself or for both. Both sides profit sustainably from that!

Moreover, you also benefit your mentor. You should definitely consider how and with what you can provide a *gratuitous* benefit for him so that it will, in fact, be a win-win relationship.

Always think about a win-win relationship and act accordingly. Then you will receive practical knowledge from your mentor because the most interesting facts and the most interesting insider knowledge only come up after a certain amount of time, when mutual trust and your growth have reached a certain individual level of trust. Be patient and take your time!

Bear in mind that a mentor also needs time to assess your person with respect to your thought structure and your thought level.

Moreover, because he must also assess whether you are worth his sharing his wealth of experience and have the talent needed to implement your life vision.

Growth driver 2: Investor

Becoming an investor means investing correctly in your own future.

Consequently, I must not exchange the factor of time against money, but rather performance against money! Moreover, gainful employment does not fundamentally make you rich! By contrast, investors will inevitably become rich through transparent, multipliable systems! Today, the internet also helps further with the easy accessibility of my target group. Investments in your own website are quite inexpensive and are well suited for the start-up entrepreneur to expand his business.

Ideas and Notes on the topic investor:

_____

_____

_____

_____

_____

Growth Driver 3: Income producing actions

Always ask yourself whether that which you are currently doing is an income-producing action or not.

"The more income-producing actions that you undertake, the more income you can generate!"

Develop clarity in relationship to your vision, consider income-producing actions in your time planning and allow these actions corresponding priority. Set clear priorities in your daily actions so that clear results in the direction of your individual goals are generated and your time can be used more optimally.

Focus on income-producing actions every day and position them clearly, concretely and with consciousness of the time!

Growth Stimulator 4: Specialist

If we work determinedly and intensively on our goal, we change ourselves positively because – with every task, with every problem, which we solve on the way to our goal to develop our personality, – our personality grows! (Milestones of hindrances, chance givers)

This includes completing our tasks effectively and efficiently.

In other words, that we work on the right tasks and deal with them correctly.

Familiarize yourself with a unique selling point (for a third person), such as, for instance, your appearance as an expert or as a specialist. etc. [10]

> **"You must be an expert, then people will come to you with their problems."**

We must create a positive environment for others so that people forget their inhibitions and we must have an open mind towards all that is new, along with the right, creative thinking attitude!

---

[10] How does this work? See under Growth phase 8, correct positioning on the following pages!

Growth Driver 5: Selling

I have to develop enthusiasm for my wish, have and radiate enthusiasm so that the spark can fire! This involves unconditional trust in my abilities and a motto, such as "NGU" (Never give up), to achieve my goals.

It must be a burning desire, with trust and persistence focused on your concrete goal! Almost all successful human beings belong to the group of sellers.

In order to be able to implement your goals optimally, you should learn how to sell well. For this purpose it is, first of all, important that you be authentic in your rhetorical expression as well as in your body language. It is imperative that you learn to sell!

Growth Driver 6: Learn properly

Hereto: Read the *right* books correctly! Lifelong learning also means, that, in the best case, we focus on the goals that lie before us and prepare ourselves for the requirements relating thereto. We achieve this by concentrating on the research and the acquisition of the necessary knowledge on this!

A tip for this in advance: Also become a quick reader! Being a quick reader, i.e. books or seminars for quick readers make sense so that more information is acquired in a shorter period of time. For this purpose, only one technique is learned!

Motto for the topic of learning: Develop competencies which are beneficial for you on the way to your personal vision! Everything else is distraction or an excuse!

Growth Driver 7: Correct positioning

Approach for your benefit recipient – positioning

1. <u>Determine the problem:</u> Identify the most important problem of the recipient of your benefit, henceforth, **your** future potential benefit recipient! Put the problem in concrete terms as precisely as possible, so that you can develop a concrete solution.

2. <u>Develop a solution:</u> Ask yourself how you can solve this problem of your potential benefit recipient. Next, ask yourself with what approach and what method you want to solve the problem of your possible benefit recipient!

3. <u>Concretize the method</u>: Concretize the method, which should lead to a solution for the problem. Furthermore, define the **components** which compose your method and how you want to

communicate it in writing and verbally, clearly and understandably!

4. <u>Formulate an offer:</u> Formulate what **concrete use** your benefit recipient has from your offer! (please describe it in writing!)

5. <u>Question the use:</u> Question further on the next level which other deeper benefit your benefit recipient has from this? (Please describe in writing!)

6. <u>Find out basic needs:</u> Now consolidate it even more and ask repeatedly: On the other hand, what use does my benefit recipient have from the present survey result? What does he have concretely from this, what basic need is satisfied by this? (Please describe in writing).

Only then, have you found the **actual reason** and, with that, you have available the basic need of your benefit recipient.

Only then, have you determined how you can position yourself in the market to recognize the best possible use for your benefit recipient!

Growth Driver 8: Your own will

In a nutshell, some important parameters and steps for the factor "your own will".

Support for your will through your own vision

It should be your own personal vision; it should be your own goals, which you have laid down yourself!

Without the influence of third parties! Only in this way, is it possible to develop sustainable, intrinsic enthusiasm so that obstacles on the way to the goal can be overcome. Build up anticipation in this way!

Divide up into the areas "Where do I want to avoid pain" and "Where do I want to experience joy?"

Stay in the highest level of thinking, the creative and imaginative level! Build up a firm belief that you will achieve your vision. Don't forget to incorporate your own feelings into your vision, so that you already try to feel what it would feel like when you have achieved your goal: So, how would you feel, how would it smell and taste, how would it look, how would it sound when you have reached your goal? Address all the senses and employ them!

Make it a habit to visualize your long-term goals daily, i.e., regularly in your mind's eye, with all your senses. Set some interim goals – milestones - which indicate that you are making progress and getting closer to your vision. So that you don't lose sight of your direction, it is advisable that you write down daily, weekly, monthly, quarterly and material goals, such as marketing goals, contact goals, argumentation goals etc. to keep them continuously in focus.

Thereby, through constant verification or falsification[11] of the direction of action adhered to, our corridors of action, compliance with the goal is constantly examined.

Certainly, you won't have everything under control, however your direction, just like driving your car, is continually adaptable to the current circumstances.

In addition, ideally, you should also regularly reflect in writing, by noting your successes and breakthroughs as well as your failures and defeats and from this draw conclusions for your further course of action. Motto: Every day I will become a little better! In this way, the unfolding of my personality succeeds through constant self-reflection!

---

[11] Thus the clarification, whether it turns out through review, whether it is right or false.

Support for your will through clarity

Clarity should prevail with respect to the effort expended on the way to my vision through a determination of the cost-effectiveness:

Determine the price for your goal: What must you do, what must you do without, to achieve your goal? What are you willing to do? Then make a conscious, quick and written decision, so you can involve your will in implementing your vision right from the start!

Motto: "Everything that is taken from you, must also have been given to you beforehand." (Service vs. Trade-Off)

Supporting your will through concentration.

Optimal concentration can only be achieved if I know my goal and my vision down to the last detail! Please always focus only on one issue, on the next necessary interim goal!

Concentration on the here and now is important!

(Don't do) everything at once, but one thing after the other – step-by-step. The step-by-step method means only concentrating on one project after another in order to achieve it! You will see that this clearly brings faster and better results!

Concentration means not scattering (your efforts) but focusing (on them one at a time)! By, for instance, using the step-by-step method. Taking one step after the other is much better than doing everything at once. Multi-tasking does not bring you to your goal.

As Bismarck once said. "He who hunts many rabbits, ultimately catches none of them."

Without a goal and substance, no concentration is possible!

Find out: What brings me closer to my goal? What can deter me from my goal? Internal resistance, such as, for example, basic beliefs, habits or external obstacles - market conditions, competition, co-workers, etc...

Alertness is required here!

Therefore, you must always keep an eye on your diversions and distractions! Every distraction, every diversion means a swerving away from our goal! Distractions take us off course. When we concentrate and act more, then we reach the goal we have set for ourselves earlier. Definitely get rid of time-wasters consistently!

To counteract these, we must develop routines that benefit us.

Examples: Only read emails at three set times daily - morning, mid-day and evening. This creates free space in your head! Develop morning and evening routines, such as meditation, prepare to-do lists for each day. Gauge what is important and what is urgent and distinguish between them; develop dream albums to better visualize and always have the big goal in view!

Supporting the will by concentrating on my person

Personality: This essential factor on the way to personal and also financial independence, directly affects other people.

Focusing on the external attitude means: It is your conscious external approach, which allows your environment either to react the same way (as you do) or otherwise. Your areas of activity: optics, body language, etc.

The focus on internal attitude means the same for the internal approach. For example, with the topic of self-confidence. Self-confidence is a very important characteristic and internal attitude, as this represents the basis for every successful action. If you don't trust yourself, if you yourself don't trust anything, why should others do so?

Focus on values and actions: For third parties, reliability is the precursor to confidentiality and trust. For when we determine that there is someone there who does exactly what he says(he will do), this third party can better gauge this person, which, in turn, leads to confidentiality and, in the end, to trust:[12]

Focus on personality feedback: It is, obviously, also important that I reflect on myself regularly and observe my effect on other people! This also involves regularly inviting feedback from third parties. This is important for amending my own personality development, so that I can regulate it. For only then, when I know what my effect is, can I direct myself with respect to my thought patterns and habits and develop further.

Focus on self-optimization: Develop an aura, develop charisma! Consciously decide for a positive champion's stance, mindset and body posture!

Supporting your will through a priority list

You should first create a list for yourself so that you can determine your priorities and make a decision about what you want TO DO.

Thereby, it will also be absolutely clear WHAT you have set as a goal for yourself. Now, after you know the field of action needed, you can deduce the individual measures. You now also know what helps you to reach your goal.

---

[12] Motto: Act authentically!

So the necessary concentration on the necessary goals results! Distractions will be more visible and can now be consciously deterred.

Supporting your will through immediate application

Start! DO! Implement without a doubt that I might not be able to achieve my goal.[13] For it is up to me and when I start, then I move myself towards my goal. If I don't start, it is guaranteed: Nothing!

Starting and acting directly means that you are now transforming your thoughts into reality and ensuring an external effect. Hereby, your thoughts are situated in reality and create reactions in your environment. Thus your engagement is "in play". Bring your will into reality! Be a "doer" instead of a "refrainer"! Actively decide and act immediately. One method for this: Observe the 72-hour-rule.[14] Moreover, don't ask "whether" it will happen but "how" it will happen.[15]

---

[13] Motto: God helps those who help themselves

[14] Motto for the three day or 72-hours-rule: That which you do not begin in three days you automatically put off! Thus, as soon as my goal is determined and concretely formulated in writing, it should be begun immediately, if possible within 72 hours!

[15] With "how", solutions are sought automatically!

First On Top Milestone – Your own will

Now, you have also gotten acquainted

with tools that support your will,

which can be helpful in

implementing your project.

Acquire these characteristics and

these supports by using one tool every day.

Do this so long and on a revolving basis until

these tools are so programmed into your

subconscious that they run unconsciously

and have become recognizable as a habit.

Motto for this: Practice makes perfect!

Growth Driver 9 Perseverance

"Never-give-up – Method"

Obstacles represent milestones on the way to your success and are also a part of it.

Obstacles are there either to be gotten out of the way or to evade and seek another way.

Therefore, it is important that you seek and find your personal approach, in order to deal with these experience phases. Show your teeth! Work on your intrinsic motivation through systematic maintenance of your motivation, which also helps to start again in times of crisis! This happens through the development of your life vision, your big picture!

Publicize your project!

Share your plan with third parties! Then, there is no going back. The question then is no longer *if* you will complete your project successfully, but you concentrate only on the *how*.

Personal Mastery!

For you, personal mastery means not only that you don't give up as soon as obstacles are put in the way, but that you develop a master plan with a master key and characteristics, such as "hanging on", also called persistence or discipline, which will bestow a successfully lived life on you and your environment.

Only with these experiences on your way to the goal, towards your vision, will you become the personality whom you must be in order to make your future purpose in life become a reality.

And, to develop yourself into the person, into the human being, who can also live out your dreams of today in the future.

Growth Driver 10 Time (Efficiency)

Use your time correctly by thinking big

"It takes the same amount of time whether I think about 500 Euros or more than 50,000 Euros income."

Use your time correctly by thinking long-term

Developing long-term thinking means being aware that we often overestimate what, for example, we can achieve in one year and mostly underestimate what can be accomplished in 5 or 10 years. Champions are aware that we need long-term development in order to implement big goals. Therefore, never give up, despite what obstacles you must overcome or clear away!

Use your time by thinking in a focused way.

Concentration on your goal and blocking out distractions.

Read and learn from books on self- and time-management, which deal with purposeful time-management (compass or direction planning).

> Impulse: "Experience is either learning or winning!"

Perception exercise: No failure is possible

This exercise serves to make clearer how you think about things, your view of things. Am I a doubter? Is this why I don't begin this or another project? Do I not trust myself due to my experiences? Could it be different than I imagine it to be? Do I have more chances with another perspective, with another approach?

The exercise "No failure possible!" should make this clear for you. Let's assume that a fairy would help you today so that nothing you wanted to do could go wrong. What would you do if you knew for certain that nothing could go wrong? If you had all the resources available, if money did not play a role? Which project would you immediately begin?

_____

_____

_____

_____

_____

_____

_____

Now write down why you have doubts, that (without a good fairy) you cannot carry out this project, that it would fail. Explain your doubts and challenge this on facts that obstruct your project.

_____

_____

_____

_____

_____

_____

_____

_____

Do you notice that much of this takes place only in your head, in your mindset? Afterwards, try to find arguments, which could dispel your doubts!   Keep trying to find further arguments, which could help speak for success and against obstacles? In this way, you can clear away your doubts, little by little. Determine the chances for your project and focus on this!

_____

_____

_____

_____

_____

_____

_____

_____

Second On Top Milestone – Failure impossible

Now you have accomplished

the next On-Top Milestone.

It is now clear how crucially

important your thinking,

your basic attitude is for achieving your goals.

If you don't believe that you are going to achieve your goal, you will also not achieve it.

If, however, you are convinced that you will achieve your goal, you will also manage it.

Your attitude is crucial for which result you obtain!

Without a goal, no hits!

Defining my milestones to a successful implementation of my finely adjusted life vision.

"If you have no life vision that you yearn for, towards which you work, which you want with all your heart to achieve, then there is possibly also no motive to make an effort. [16]

---

[16] Cf.: Erich Fromm; German-American psychoanalyst, philosopher and social psychologist, who advocated for humanistic, democratic socialism (ca. 1920)

Goals describe the way to our personal life vision.

Goals are binding designated **milestones** on the way to our vision.

Thanks to the previous exercises, you are now fully aware of and clearly recognize that when you believe in your goals, you can also achieve them. You can determine the path of your goals by planning from your vision up to the present time. If, for example, your vision, with a focus on ten years in the future, meets your expectations, you can create a time plan from this state in the future back to the present. Ideally, you would do this with a time axis in which you record the milestones that need to be completed and, thereby, make the way to your future predictable. Here, both the substance as well as temporal factors should be determined in advance if you want to reach the interim goal on the way to your vision. Your goals should have the following parameters in order to guarantee realistic implementation.

First, you goals should be significant, thereby meaningful and crucial for you. Therefore, for implementation it is important that your goals be clearly defined.

Furthermore, your goals should be predictable. The criteria which should be fulfilled, must be calculated in advance and be verifiable.

Moreover, your goal should be desirable and attractive for you personally.

Then it is also important to give some thought to the implementation realities of your goal. Here, your goal should be adapted to your skills and abilities, in particular so that you know what you can preferably delegate to other people who can do it better than you can.

Finally, a feasible goal must also be brought into connection with the time-factor now. The question is, when do you want to achieve the goal you have set? In the end, a fixed date for when you want to reach your goal must be determined.

Only she, who knows her goal, finds her way!

Laozi[17]

---

[17] Laozi, the legendary philosopher, who is said to have lived in the 6th Century before Christ. Depending on the transcription, his name is also written as Lao-Tzu or Lao-Tze

Clarity through measuring my personal success?

On what do I measure my personal success? An example of action on this would be that you determine the milestones and keep a record of the successes!

Success amplifier: Keep the focus on the goal! Fix your focus on that which you want: Your goals!

Thus it is important that you write down your goals, for writing is more powerful, more sustainable and more transparent and thus gives clarity to your goals!

This clarity makes your goals concrete and, thereby, feasible for your subconscious!

Hereby, it also helps that you concretize your goals in a way – if possible - that they can also be calculated in order to guarantee better implementation and to present the partial steps in an understandable and conceivable way. Thus, I also achieve better planning security.

Define your goal clearly:

_____

_____

_____

_____

_____

_____

_____

_____

_____

Is the goal measureable?

_____

_____

_____

_____

_____

_____

_____

_____

_____

Goal vs. Implementation reality:

_____

_____

_____

_____

_____

_____

_____

_____

_____

Fixed date for the goal:

_____

_____

_____

_____

_____

_____

_____

_____

_____

_____

_____

3. On Top Milestone – Monitoring success

Monitoring success is necessary with

respect to your goals, so that you

Don't lose sight of your goals and

vision and so that you can record and

also celebrate your partial successes,

your milestones on the way to your vision,

Yes, that's right, life should also be fun!

Celebrate your successes. Here too, the way is the goal!

For on the way to your vision, you develop yourself into the person who is able to live your future vision. Prepare a timeline in which you record your milestones, one after the other, so that you can always determine visually how you are coming closer to your vision, step by step.

Growth driver 11: Success comes through action!

The secret of making progress is simple:

You must only begin immediately!

For: If you don't do anything, nothing will happen!

Tell yourself:

I. I must become a **doer**! Simply act!. Don't brood or ramble, but simply do, for, in the worst case, it will be experience! Only those have already lost, who do not begin to work on their future, who don't act!

II. I must take over the **responsibility** myself! i.e., I must concentrate on my goal and not allow myself to be held back by any obstacles!

III. Make **decisions!** And **DO!** Why is that so important? Because making decisions quickly brings us closer to action and does not thwart us in our inner dialogue!

IV. **Doubts** cannot arise and if they do, they will be ignored through our actions

V. **"Try"** is something for negative, non-acting people because they expect obstacles that they cannot resolve! Successful people do everything in their power to reach their goal! **No Plan B!**

My ideas and notes on the successful implementation of
my personal vision:

_____

_____

_____

_____

_____

_____

_____

_____

LAST BUT NOT LEAST

"He who gives up freedom to have more security, has neither freedom nor security!"

Benjamin Franklin

„Plan concretely and carefully for hope is not a strategy when your welfare is at stake!"

Do your want to dream your dreams or live your dreams?

It is your decision between a rat race or a life in freedom!

It is entirely in your hands in the here and now...

Warm regards

Dr. Norbert Hermann

I wish you the right decision, energetic action and all the best!

Go4BetterLife Concept – Secret of Success: Personality

Impulse-Day-Seminar

Your breakthrough into a successful, self-determined future through systematic personality development.

- How you create or hold back your orientation with your own vision of the future
- How you arrive where you really want to go
- How you achieve the breakthrough to your own goals through focusing on the target.
- How you gain security and confidence

- How you obtain important impulses for the development of a successful and balanced personality
- Get to know your success accelerator
- Get to know your self-saboteur
- How you proceed with the correct strategy
- How you achieve the right attitude
- How you can achieve your dream life

Recognize: What has really kept you from achieving your personal goals so far?

Further seminar information and dates can be found at:

www.drnorberthermann.com

Do you have questions about the seminar? Request further information at: kontakt@drnorberthermann.com

Instagram: drnorberthermann